Life What Eventually Matters

Tony and Anthony Ravello

Published by Universalghostwriter, 2023.

While every precaution has been taken in the preparation of this book, the publisher assumes no responsibility for errors or omissions, or for damages resulting from the use of the information contained herein.

LIFE WHAT EVENTUALLY MATTERS

First edition. July 26, 2023.

Copyright © 2023 Tony and Anthony Ravello.

ISBN: 979-8891845657

Written by Tony and Anthony Ravello.

Table of Contents

....1

Chapter 1: The Birth of Meaning 5

Chapter 2: The Odyssey of Life.. 11

Chapter 3: The Complexity of Human Emotions........................... 17

Chapter 4: Humans vs. Animals.. 23

Chapter 5: Human vs. Human 30

Chapter 6: Battles within 35

Chapter 7: Seeking Meaning.. 44

Chapter 8: The End of Everything: Death................................ 50

WHAT EVENTUALLY HAPPENS IN LIFE

About the Author

Anthony Ravello, hailing from Trinidad and Tobago, has had a life journey of exploring spirituality and growing as a person. He went to Siparia Boys Roman Catholic School, where he learned about Roman Catholicism and developed a strong connection with God. Anthony drifted away from his childhood beliefs in his twenties, but life eventually led him to a new path. Now, he's part of a non-denominational Church that focuses on the teachings of Jesus Christ. They believe that water baptism shows faith in Jesus—a way to express beliefs and obey His example of life, death, and rebirth.

At 67, Anthony's view is inclusive, imagining heaven without divisions between religious groups. He envisions harmony among all souls, whether Catholic, Methodist, or others. Anthony's story reflects growing faith, personal changes, and the power of spirituality on life's journey.

Chapter 1: The Birth of Meaning

Often do we wonder how we have lived on this green rock ball for so long? Why are we living, dreaming, and dozing instead of our fellow brethren? The concept of time that we know and believe is infinite, a never-ending cycle that goes beyond human comprehension. From our Birth to Death, we ponder upon the question of our very translational and glorious existence, whether our birth has a hidden meaning behind it or we just exist.

We are born through the process of human fertilization, where two people, a male, and a female, meet and have sexual intercourse. The male semen containing million of sperms races through the fallopian tubes of the female uterus and encounters its final destination, "The Egg" It is at this point that the sperm looks around and finds that out of his millions of brethren, only a few stand, panting, their vision is clear, and destination is one. And so begins the final struggle, and with the will of the thousands of mountains and the fury of great kings, they breach the wall known as "Zona Pellucida" Once the sperm breaches the wall, no additional soldiers are granted any entry. The 'glorious' sperm becomes the chosen one. Now the sperm looks around once more to ensure the well-being of his brethren, but all it finds around itself are its fallen comrades. However, the will lives on, and with honor, the sperm hits the egg, and so begins the formation of a human being. In short, fertilization occurs, the female becomes pregnant within 24 hours, the chromosomes are traded, and nine months later, a loud yet small human is finally birthed, named, and through the will of God, lives.

This is the over-dramatization of the beginning of the small, fragile, insignificant, significant, strong, and vast phenomenon we call life. What bugs and ridicules the reasoning of moral beings on this planet is whether our existence is pre-ordained or a mere coincidence. There is no telling with precision how old this planet has been in existence or how long the glorified, celebrated, prideful, and self-centered humans have been in existence. However, many from different backgrounds, beliefs, and knowledge have a say in it.

But before we tread on a journey of finding meaning in our existence, we shall know well who these groups of people are. The grave importance of those who hold the major voice of the 'moral being' is the religious groups who believe in a deep and profound meaning of human existence and believes that an entity, a greater force, pre-ordains human life. There are scientists who believe in their knowledge. They devote their time to seeking knowledge backed by scientific findings. Finally, there are philosophers who devote their time to seeking wisdom through reasoning and principles of Virtues.

In light of religion, humans have obeyed and prayed to many Gods. Some found God in stones, and some found God in humans, while for some, God is a concept, a never seen entity. If we begin counting religions, we will be lost in time, history, and eventually incomplete data. With countless civilizations, there can be no number to give even a ballpark estimation of how many religions there have been.

With the rise, fall, and evolvement of civilization, religions also evolved; however, through our history, there are some which remained with us, and these become major wide known religions to mankind, and many believed to be the truth of it all, the truth of our human existence and meaning. Christianity, Islam, Judaism, Hinduism, and Buddhism have been around for centuries, and while other religions were lost with time, only these remained, with millions of followers around the world.

In Christianity, humans are born in the image of God. This means that every individual is a unique creation of God and lives to serve a purpose. Highlighting a human birth with no meaning is rejected by Christians. Everyone that ever lived their birth, existence, and death was pre-destined by God. Similarly, Muslims believe that our lives have meaning, and so do our birth which was pre-ordained by God, a higher force.

People who believe in religions have a strong faith in the reasoning of our existence. Everything that ever lived served a greater purpose, even the smallest of living things invisible to our naked eye, a bacterium. A bacterium has many purposes, one of many is to fight harmful bacteria and ensure our well-being. A healthy lifestyle is maintained, and the air around us that we breathe makes this planet habitable. Every creation of God performs its duty. No creation sits idly and contributes nothing. Such is the beauty of life; even by doing nothing, something greater beyond words is contributed that all beings, living or non, take advantage of. Obeying a religion makes it an obligation to cherish what is around us, and when and with the cherishing of life that surrounds us, we become subjected to appreciate what we have. First and foremost, our existence, the realization that life has value, and that the creator ordered our existence, and with his grace, we walked and breathed the Earth.

From a scientific perspective, there is no inherent meaning to the concept of a divine being. A scientist might have their own beliefs, be that religion or atheism. However, we can find proof of a divine being by diving deep into scientific discoveries. Birth, fertilization, and embryonic formation prove that our genetics and birth define our characteristics and traits. The uniqueness of a human becomes inevitable. Biology makes us unique individuals, and the formation of our cells, physical characteristics, and personality traits all prove divine existence.

We have the whole universe explained to us, and the existence of such miracles around us from something as small as bacteria and as vast as space makes us cling to the belief that a greater force keeps things in their place. However, it can be argued that whether or not that force has the demands from people of spiritual beliefs say so. Looking deep into the trajectory of our existence and the universe, worshipping a greater force is gratitude; obedience to its commands is a code to a wise life.

From a philosophical point of view, many philosophers presented their theories on the meaning behind the birth of a human. Philosophers engage in the reasoning behind human existence and seek the reasoning as to why we behave in ways that are beyond comprehension. They explore the principles of reasoning, the nature of our existence, and the ethics of virtues. Philosophy is age-old and is still practiced. There is a wealth of knowledge, but each philosopher presented their own set of ideas and theories. Similarly, the concept of birth is no stranger to the meaning behind the birth of a human.

Socrates is a legend in the world of philosophers, the father of Western philosophy. Socrates believed that the soul existed before birth and that before we drew our first breath, we were conscious, and it was not until we were born did we forget our inherent knowledge of the truth. It is a debate whether Socrates believed in religious ideas, but after a deeper look at his writings, it can be said he respected the ideas of Greek gods. From Socrates' theory alone, we can align different beliefs together. There is an idea of a soul that exists before birth and remains in existence after we depart from our physical body. We were somewhat chosen to live, and it was beyond our control.

Jean-Paul Sartre also has a say in human existence, and he intelligently named it concisely and called it "Existentialism" In his theory, he debated that we exist here and now and that it is what we do that truly defines us. Our choices give our life a purpose that everyone believes to be true. His framework's central ideas were based on our existence in the mortal body. In existentialism, we give birth to our truth. There is no pre-destined divine truth, but it doesn't exist unless we make it. For a man like Sartre, there was no God, and life had no inherent purpose. In Sartre's world, man has freedom, and he should seek knowledge and give his life true meaning. No pre-destiny to give us moral duty.

Philosophers are geniuses, and we study them in schools and universities. Whether we agree or disagree, we continue to respect their ideologies as it gives us the freedom to acquire knowledge and dare us to seek the truth and see the universe from our perspective. Even among the reasoning of philosophers themselves, there are contradictions; however, we cannot fully neglect those theories.

Anyone who believes in God knows that we have 'free will.' That's how the concept of right and wrong and good and evil is birthed. Our *dear*

Ami theory of existentialism is somewhat agreeable for pupils of God as we do have control of what we do. God has given us control of our life. We are responsible for what we do. Similarly, by mixing the ideas of Socrates and Sartre on our meaning of birth, we will stumble upon the ideology of religion. Before we are born, our purpose is given. We know the truth, and upon birth, we forget our purpose and live to seek it again through our free will.

There is a story that I was told when I was a kid. Our whole life is a staged drama we perform, and eventually, just as the curtains unroll, they roll back in. The whole of life, a play, becomes a small, staged drama; in the end, everything ceases to exist. From the perspective of this staged play, our birth plays a significant role and is worth pondering.

How do we come to play the role? Was it something that we were destined to play? Or was it sheer luck? Just like many before us, that came played their respective roles. It must be noted that our life, our role, does make an impact, no matter how small that is. If it were anyone else who would've played that role, it would've been quite different. A small change in the dialogue would've reflected an entirely different performance. The director and the producers chose us because they deemed us fit for the role of a lifetime. Of course, some people could've played the same role as we did, but they would have performed through their judgments. In short, an entirely different version, an entirely different story. We born to play that role.

Chapter 2: The Odyssey of Life

Each individual grows up to have their own set of beliefs. Our beliefs are important. They give us a sense of purpose, a will to strive, and prove our rights. Anyone who lives with no belief becomes a purposeless wanderer, but unfortunately, humanity comes with pride. We become too aware of ourselves and enforce our version of truth onto others to prove our worth. We do this so often that we become blinded by our version of the truth, our truth that abandons any reason, and that is how the world becomes filled with corruption and war.

In simplicity, there is some truth in our lies, and there is some lie in our truth. That's how things are. We are the middlemen in the time of the universe, neither in hell nor in heaven. Our purpose is to be the best version of ourselves with the knowledge we acquire and not what we are given. We should neither make this world a living heaven nor a hell, and it is only by trying to achieve the heavenly charm in this world have we strike an imbalance. We should be aware of everything. We should have the knowledge of humankind within us, and with that knowledge, we should seek the truth that we believe with our sanity and implement that in our lives first and then those around us.

Looking deep within ourselves, we know that we yearn for knowledge and peace. In our most lonely moments, we tell ourselves that we ought to be the best version of ourselves and that we should live to make this world a better place. But how do we make this world a better place? How do we find the meaning of our birth that we forgot upon drawing our first breath? Or how do we find meaning in our birth when we are born with no purpose? Isn't it our right to give our life a purpose, if we don't have any? Shouldn't we make use of our cognitive abilities? Change comes from within. It is always the smallest things that we do that make a ladder elevate to a better view.

Understanding oneself is the first step to revolutionizing the world and ourselves for a better life, striking a balance between heaven and hell. Before I dive deep into the spiritual realms of our fragile yet powerful minds, I find it necessary to explain what the balance of heaven and hell is. Why am I fixated on abandoning heaven on Earth? How sinister of me to be blaspheme against peace. Let me explain. We believe that heaven, hell, and our life in the middle is the creation of God. That is the resemblance between the three. Heaven, hell, and Earth are all filled with people, the creation of God. In heaven and hell, there is no free will. There is no voice. They are the lasting results of our actions. We have no power over what happens in there as God doesn't give that power to us. It is solely for him to decide what happens there. However, God gave us the power of what happens within here, the temporal home of middlemen.

Heaven and hell are a place of acceptance. We abandon our struggles to prove our worth. We rid ourselves of war, money, and fame. It is the answer to our purposes. In heaven, there is the laughter of a blissful eternity. In hell, there is an anguish of a tormented eternity. Here, there is a catharsis of the delusional eternity. The reason this place must be and is a balance of both is we are not singular; we are born with different ideals and morals. We live with our own version of the truth that we created. Wars are fought to conquer the land, to expand, but it is also fought to take what's yours, rightfully, to protect those who are being killed by intruders. In heaven, there is no war and hatred. In a court, a rapist or a murderer cannot be pardoned or forgiven. It is important to punish them so a lesson is learned and fear is imposed. In hell, there is no court. We fight wars and do not forgive those who do not deserve it. We pass judgment without a shred of mercy, all because it is necessary to run things with ease, to maintain order among orderless.

In this limbo of heavenly-hell, we live and breathe, we walk and run, we mourn and cry, and we learn and grow. With a small amount of time attached to our life, we develop ourselves to become the best version of ourselves. We have no control over life and death. We do not know with surety when we will draw our last breath. However, we have labeled the stages of our teensy-weensy life.

There are six stages of life that are generally accepted by all. Each stage has unique characteristics and traits. Infancy, Childhood, Adolescence, Young Adulthood, Middle Adulthood, and Late Adulthood are the six stages that we experience from birth to death. Death, if we are old and wrinkly enough to carry a crane with us and are consumed in these stages.

These stages have their own distinctive personalities, and although it is quite possible to remain consistent in these stages, those who do are 'fools' and 'ignorant'. Who would want to stay the same throughout their lives? It just doesn't make sense. Our life is short. Ask a man who got his foot down his grave about how long was it? Is he tired? And I guarantee it they'll say they've only just begun. I remember being in my 30s, and it was our annual college friends meet-up, me and this good ol' friend of mine who was very drunk that particular night.

He put a cigarette between his lips tenderly as I lit it up. Poor guy was too wasted to light it up himself, and as he began to smoke, he went, "I still think about her?"

"Who?" I asked cluelessly.

"My Angela," he replied with his dim voice filled with shame. At this point, I had no idea who he was talking about. He wasn't married, nor was he in a relationship with anyone. I know it was someone from high school since we were together in high school. This friend of mine back in school was quite carefree. All he wanted was to have fun with his mates. He was extremely good at sports. Unlucky for us, every girl we liked had a crush on him they were too consumed in him to give us their even undivided attention. I sat in silence with him as he smoked, going back to my not-so-reliable memory, and there it hit me.

"OH SHIT! Angela, the tall brunette girl from our history class?" I almost shouted. How could I forget her? Every guy wanted to be with her, I thought to myself. "Yeah, Angela, what about her? You two dated for like a few months, and broke up, right?”

"Not really, we did break up though, but we started dating back again, and eventually, we broke up over the silliest thing ever," he said. "What was it?" I asked. "She fell out of love," he said with a smile as he continued intoxicating his lungs with his dear cigarette he looked at with care.

"Isn't it the silliest thing ever? How could you fall out of love? How is it possible that we have only a limited amount of love to give? If that's the case, then I believe there is no God. Either that, or this is God's punishment for us for our sins," he continued, and each word he uttered carried with it the guilt of shame and regret. I wondered if what he was saying was really the truth. I was still naïve back then to answer him. So, I just put my hand on his shoulder and said stupidly, “Forget about it. She just got bored. No such thing as running out of love.”

Now that I have lived to be 67 years old, I would have answered differently. I would have consoled him even though I still believe in the second part. Blaming it all on love doesn't justify it. Love doesn't just exist in the air. We give birth to it. There is a need within us, and thus our pursuit begins until we finally find it or fate decides its time, and once we do, we protect. Love is just an emotion. It is we who give meaning to it by cherishing it.

Back when we met, we were 35, busy living to make enough money and buy ourselves the nicest car. My friend, broken by Angela, felt that he still was 24. He said he was the happiest at that age and believed he had reached the highest level of happiness he could have achieved. Unfortunately, without realizing it, he was living off Angela's silly idea of running out of emotions. He simply ran out of happiness. Tragic, he despised and mocked the idea of running out of love, and yet unconsciously, he was doing it. In his mind, he still was 24. He stopped living once Angela left him.

Life is full of tragedy, disappointment, and struggles. We are hopeless romanticists, tormented strugglers, and crude failures at every stage of life, from infancy to late adulthood. We are bound to be these hapless creatures of God. In infancy, we drag our bodies to crawl with every ounce of the strength of the Spartans and the blood of Zeus to learn to walk. We desperately try to be in the arms of our first love, Mother. Our mother becomes our only comfort giving us the health and love that we so much yearn and cry for. However, we do constantly take loads of shit, thanks to whoever hero came up with diapers. I really think if not for diapers, there would be a smaller number of children in the world. As we grow, our enthusiasm towards romance, our ferocity towards struggles, and our growth towards failure take a drastic change in our life. It becomes more serious and severe. We realize that life without a care for our well-being will put us in situations of standing at the edge of a cliff while Wild Bill stands on the other side with his sadistic gun pointed at us. This is not the end yet. You can charge at

Wild Bill at full speed or jump off the cliff. Trust me; you will survive because that's what we have been doing so far. Say your prayer and run your marathon.

We will lose people, we will be betrayed, we will die, and we will live again and again till our breath runs out, but above all, we will change. We look within ourselves and see that we have been making mistakes. Our jobs, our love, our family, and our home will all perish, and at the end, we will stand before God, telling him what torment befall us and how we fought a battle we were losing. We gotta keep moving forward, carrying the dead on our shoulders and dragging the things we once lost.

Chapter 3: The Complexity of Human Emotions

We are complex creatures, composed by a divine being, roaming the Earth, and sometimes with our inborn and hard-to-hide curiosity, we fly out to space to find a hint of life out there to justify with sincerity that we are miserably bored and alone. Alone, even with fellow humans, animals, plants, and viruses among us. With so much around us, we still need more to fill a void inside of us. A closer inspection of our miserably grand life will result in us pondering about the pitiful circumstances we are in. We are bored to death and feel as if we have felt and experienced everything there is to feel, touch, breathe, and experience. Insufficient, we wonder if there wasn't enough for us to be excited about. In all actuality, it's not the fault of an animal or our friends that we are bored but ours. We are bored with ourselves and our very own marvelous life all because our emotions are boring.

If only we had control over our emotions, wouldn't our lives be easier? After all, we wouldn't be bored. We wouldn't have our hearts broken over that one girl that stopped time for us, and above all, we wouldn't have made a total fool out of ourselves. Our silly emotions had us feeling things and making us unbelievably cruel, foolish, empathetic, and so much more we despise ourselves for.

We are crueler than we are kind. We are cruel when we should've been kinder and kind when we should have been not tyrannically but sympathetically cruel. So, with my sincerest apologies, let me say it again we are bored simply because we do not understand ourselves. Our emotions doesn't bore us they just dull us to see the truthfulness of the world but take away the emotions, and we will be deadbeats waiting to draw our last breath. Human Emotions are complex and hard to understand or maybe they are impossible to understand. Our whole life is just a show where the audience seems uninterested as we try and prove how our emotions are justifiable.

Every day I go through a rollercoaster of emotions I can't decide what emotions I am in as one moment, I am feeling happy and another I am taken away by the misery of my sadness. Here is an easy or, should I say, complex state of emotions I go through every day. As I wake up in the morning, I am taken away with a trippy feeling of grumpiness for reasons I can't explain. Why do I feel so grumpy? Also, it's hard for me to understand how people wake up in the morning with a broad smile. As a matter of fact, I'm not too fond of those movies where the protagonist wakes up stretching her arms out with a cunning smile on their looking-all-pretty face. It never made any sense to me. I am over 60, and never have I in those fruitful years have once woken up like that. Usually, it's me looking homeless and I am not the one to complain; I am quite happy with my life, but for as long as I can remember, I have always been grumpy waking up. A breakfast later, I am hopeful and just as I step outside, my screaming neighbour makes me hate humans. Maria, it's 10 AM, what could your poor husband possibly do to make you so angry? The air makes me worried, and the loud sound of honking cars makes my head hurt. At this point, I am on the verge of my insanity; nothing makes any sense, and I am ready to start a rebellion against the government. I casually start walking to plot the rebellion.

I am usually thinking something like a French Revolution. It was a classic show of power, but I still need supporters, but given the frustration of people, I don't suppose it to be impossible it's not so hard to achieve.

Anyways just as I am walking and plotting, I go to this locally small café for my evening coffee. I take out my pen and paper to write down some pointers (I am quite serious about the revolution), but just as I click my pen, I am interrupted by the giggles of young couples. It is at this point that I put my pen down and sip my warm coffee, and my emotions take a 180-degree turn. It makes me truly happy knowing that they are so in love. At that moment, time stops for me as I listen to the beautiful full-of-life laughs of these careless people. I start wondering how beautiful it is that they are 'in the moment'. For them, they have neither any past nor any future. It is just the moment they are in, truly living. Who knows what life has ahead of them? Will they be together, or will they be strangers? But for those, it doesn't matter they don't have to think about their past or future their present makes them happy so they enjoy it. Then during my walk in the park, I watch families walk by with their babies, and it makes me wonder how amazing life is. Will this kid remember that his parents took him out to a park every day? Watching a teenager on a sidewalk with his guitar singing Bob Dylan's "Mr Tambourine Man" with dreams of performing in front of a crowd of millions or is the joy enough for him that hopeless men like me are listening to him. Coming across a waitress serving hungry people for little tips, so she could pay her rent and focus on becoming an actor. Does she, too, with her pretty face, dream of becoming an actor like Meryl Streep?

What starts as a miserable day for me is soon taken away by little beautiful things that are not even part of my life. That struggling teenager with his crapped-up guitar singing his heart out makes my day. It is bizarre that something that is not related to me makes me happy. I used to think that because of my emotions, I was weak, constantly making mistakes and making my life more miserable. But now that I am old enough, the realization has hit me hard like a 16-wheeler truck that it was only emotions that have made me strong. Whenever I am in control of my emotions, I am taken away by my hatred and selfish desires, and when I have no control over my emotions, I am happy through my selfless desires. My day at the start is full of undesirable emotions, which makes me, really deep in my heart with a faint voice, question my existence which is soon overruled by a series of bewitchingly strange and beautiful emotions that make me want to dance on the moon. Emotions that I consider undesirable are meaningful, and if not for them, I wouldn't learn to appreciate little things like the couples at lunch or the next Bob Dylan.

As human beings, we are complete for who we are. However, our choices somewhat make us incomplete, and we then spend the rest of our lives trying to fill what's empty inside us. Emotions are beautiful, but we should be careful of how we portray them as lot meets their doom when uncontained by their emotions. When I was a kid, I had a friend whose father was quite an angry person. Whenever I would stay over at his house, I would always hear him arguing and complaining. As a kid, I was always afraid of him, and so was his son, my friend. I did not like him. His attitude towards things was problematic. Seriously, so what if the food is a little cold, you will not die is you ate cold food? I'd tell myself that when I grow up, I will never be like him. I would shut up and appreciate things and be happy with what and how it's served. His father passed away when I was 26 in another state. I remember when he gave me the news, the first thing that came to my mind was, how did he go? Was he angry? Was he complaining? I associated his whole life with anger.

I am pretty sure the man was sane just as I was, I realized that because in my 30s, I, too, was constantly complaining. I was frustrated with my job and was pissed half the time because I dreamt of being rich by the time I was 30, but I was as broke as ever, struggling to make ends meet. Like my friend's father, there were others who would always show themselves to be happy and always laughing, but later I would find that they assaulted people. Take Robin Williams. Everyone loved him for his jokes and kind nature. I associated him with the emotions of happiness, and when I heard the news of his death and later found it was suicide, it broke my heart. I cried that day. How could he be sad? He made the world laugh, and they all loved him. It bothered me a lot, and it still saddens me when I think about him. He was a beautiful man who helped the whole world. But I still associate him with happiness, such was his work and life. We will always be indebted to Robin for making the whole world laugh.

Our impressions of people are generated through the emotions they portray. Happy people are desirable. We tend to want to spend time with them, as is the case for funny; however, we try to keep our distance from people who seem angry and sad. We want to surround ourselves with positive things, which is a good thing because positive things make us happy. Unfortunately, our perception of things is mostly false. Our association of emotions with a person is one of those cases. We all have different emotions stored inside of us that we portray. We are sad, happy, excited, angry, joyous, fearful, and whatnot, but some of our emotions have a tighter hold on us, dictating us and our reasoning. It is important to notice the difference between the emotions we have no control over and those that dictate us. Emotions that we have no control over are natural things that we feel through our perception and senses, like when I am grumpy when I wake up or what I feel when I eat a deliciously cooked meal, but my actions are not dependent on that emotions.I should have control over my actions. If I act on emotions, such as screaming the moment I wake up or going over and kissing the chef, my emotions are dictating me. However, there is nothing wrong with kissing the chef over good food until and unless the chef is my wife.

We are moral beings who have emotions. Animals, too, have emotions, their emotions dictate them, but we are different. We are or should be more accountable. As a human, I should know what is good for me and what is not. I should realize my actions have consequences. With realization, I became wiser and learned to become a better and more beautiful person.

Tomorrow when I walk up, I will again be grumpy, but I know I will see things tomorrow, maybe another couple holding hands or a cat licking its feet that will make my day. Deep in my heart, I know that my emotions will remind me how truly beautiful it is to live. I know tomorrow will be a good day.

Chapter 4: Humans vs. Animals

How long has it been? How long have we been wandering into a small spherical ball in this enormously vast ocean of space? It's a question we have no concrete idea of how to answer. In all reality, it doesn't matter how long, we know a little of human history, how we have been walking, running, and sleeping on Earth. Earth, which is a grain of sand on the Saharan desert if we accumulate the pool of planets in space, even to state that is an understatement. This is an *estimate* that there are two trillion galaxies. The Milky Way alone is home to 100 billion planets, and we are one of those billions of planets in just one of the two trillion galaxies. These numbers are ridiculous, beyond conceivable. Such a grand scale is no *accident.* This is the work of God. God has every right to be prideful to claim to be a god and to claim that he is worthy of worship to command.

And what do we do? We deny the existence of such a being. It cannot be helped. It's our nature to be arrogantly conceitful.

The real question that we should really be concerned about is what we have contributed so far that has ignited this furiously egotistical spark of pride in us. Why the attitude? Why don't we know our place and bow down to a being that is far superior to us? While some do, others are simply arrogant. This arrogance is the result of pride. Pride blinds reason, pride births deception, and pride become delusion. After all, pride is one of the seven sins.

Is this unexplainable pride the result of the technological inventions we have made to make *our life* more fun and easier? Or have we achieved a feat so salient that it justifies our pride? Objectively it makes sense, considering who living being habituating the universe.

Our competitors are animals, while we do fantasize about aliens. Aliens are our greatest fantasy. Our obsession with aliens is indescribable. Actually no, it can be described as *narcissism.* Although hurtful, we have spent billions of dollars on movies alone about aliens, and it's safe to say it shows our most celebrated action, the action of the war. The same old story of aliens invading Earth has been used for God knows how many times, and it sells every time, and we love it. The idea of beating aliens back to space has us excited. It really shows how truly alone we are that we yearn for the idea of extra-terrestrial beings. Again, humans can't be blamed. Imagine 2 trillion galaxies that we know of yet in such a big sea space, and not putting or revealing the formidable opponent is truly tragic.

I do think it is the kindness from God that if such things exist, he keeps them hidden. God forbid if aliens decide to show up uninvited and they had powers we showed in movies, that my dear friends would be the doom of the loneliest and prideful beings known as humans. I worriedly wonder about a war between the two since I am a human who also fantasizes about aliens, and on my anxious wondering, I realize that we have no chance of winning against aliens if they are what we perceive them to be. Our nuclear weapons are nothing more than self-destructing machines. For our own benefit, I believe that we should just pretend aliens don't exist, and if they do, they have no interest in paying us a visit. I like to think that, unlike humans, aliens like to mind their own business, and they are truly clever. Having your priorities set and purpose defined is one true way to live.

Now that I have my priorities set, purpose defined, and delusions eradicated, I should set the tone for a more realistic conversation about *what eventually happens in life.* We should play the cards we are dealt with. And the cards on our table are the irresistibly cute, viciously dangerous, deadly venomous, insanely huge, incredibly fast, and gloriously royal. Yes, that's right, our competitors are animals. The answer to our pride, the bearer of our sins, the reason for our arrogance.

I wonder if we had animal-like powers. How different would the world be if I could store venom inside my body like a snake, claws and teeth like a tiger, wings like an eagle, and power like a bear? Indeed, I would be feared among humans, weak and puny humans.

Ironically for all the reasons that my sane mind could think animals be superior to us, they are not. It is such a shame that even with such amazing and unique abilities, animals do not even come close to us. We are simply *better* than them.

Despite our great pride in superiority, if we are to combat animals, we are sure to lose. Every kid at some point in their lives wondered about a war between humans and animals, and eventually, animals were victors. Kids surely are more realistic than adults. How are we supposed to win a combat against a 600-pound grizzly bear? Surely with our guns, we do have the upper hand, but apart from the rusty sarcasm, we have no chance against any predator. Wait, no, if a 6 feet tall 1000-pound godly strengthened herbivore buffalo charges us with might, they will pierce our body in half in just one stroke. So, it's not really a matter of herbivores or carnivores.

Predators, herbivores, omnivores, reptiles, mammals, insects, and fishes all hold the power to kill us in an instant; however, with tools, we can emerge as victors. Tools that animals do not have. Whether it is a lion, elephant, or any other animal with a weapon, we are indispensable. Today, we have forged weapons that are so dangerously powerful that we can wipe off a continent from Earth. But it is only through time that we have created weapons that made us so powerful. In ancient times weapons we had were swords and spears, which we made for the purpose of defending and hunting. As the hunting and defending continued, the realization came like a revelation that we should just kill. And thus began our never-ending entertainment of dueling with animals. We built the Colosseum to duel with animals, and as if that wasn't enough, the Romans even built training schools for gladiators to practice. Eventually, a weapon of our creation was our go-to for survival and superiority over animals.

But is that our definition of superiority? Is war necessary? The assertion of dominance through physical force has been our pathway to superiority. We are told the tales of God and myths that asserted dominance through their immaculate strength, like Zeus, Hercules, Ares, Gilgamesh, and many more. Why do animals have to carry the sins of our pride? Why should any weak being be burdened with such a horrendous act? Any wise man with morality knows that strength is not power; it is not the symbol of superiority. War and combat have proved beneficial only when fought with a purpose when all doors of conversation are locked, but even so, it only makes sense when fought with humans. We will, in detail, discuss the tragedies of war in later chapters, but animals do not fall in the same category of human morality.

We have the ability to reason, think, and act with morality. We communicate, build and adapt. Our purpose is far greater than that of animals, and by no means are we in competition with animals. Being stuck in this sphere of hope with living beings other than humans, we began comparing ourselves with animals after all the aliens did refuse to greet us. Our loneliness bound us to the 2-dimensional comparison structure because we are bored beyond compensation.

Our purpose is not the same as animals. It is more than eating and reproducing. We have the power of morality within us. Morality is a gift from God and the sinners that we are; our purpose is just to maintain morality. It is no easy feat to achieve, and that alone makes us superior in all of our creations. Free will is powerful, and if used wrong, it leads one astray.

The rule of life has always been simply that the most responsible is the most powerful. Since the dawn of men, power has always resided in those who have the highest responsibility. The King holds the highest authority in a man's world. He is responsible for his people, so he deploys men to fight wars and conquers land. He gives his people a safe land to live in freedom, and so his people obey him. In a democratic world, we have presidents who oversee the entire country. If the well-being of the country is compromised, the president is answerable for it. Even the highest paying jobs in our businesses are those who hold the responsibility. It comes down to the simple jurisdiction, which is responsibility is superiority.

Given our responsibility and moral obligation, we are no longer in comparison with animals. The whole spectrum of comparison came only with the theory of evolution. The theory summarized that all species shared a common ancestor, and humans evolved from ape-like species. The things a human is capable of doing with its intellect any other being cannot even conceive of doing, and this distinction is the characterization of the moral things we have done.

Just as we live and pride ourselves on morality, our shamed immorality also falls in the aspect of the differentiation of the two. When the power of morality was bestowed, the risk was immorality also lurked in the human consciousness. The atrocities of mankind are shameful. The sins we carry on our shoulders are heavier than the black hole. The killing, lying, fornication, and injustice we have done with the passage of time are so regrettably shameful.

The famously overrated statement *Like an animal*, whenever someone performs an inhumane act, is yet another worse sin of a human. Comparing humans with animals is a great insult inflicted on animals. Animals would never participate in mass murder, yet we have this terrible audacity to compare. We have the power to be better, but in reality, animals are the ones better than us.

Chapter 5: Human vs. Human

I sometimes wonder how we would describe humans in one word. Perhaps as bragged earlier, we can call ourselves intellectuals. But considering the record of the atrocities, betrayal, and filth we have unleashed upon this innocent world, I don't believe describing ourselves as intellectual beings would be any fair. Given that we do possess intellectual wisdom within ourselves, maybe calling ourselves genius would be fair. It is a justified reference to what we have done so far in the world with our genius minds. That is, after all, we have done tremendously pretentious things that have elevated the pursuit of our comfort, but with our genius minds, we do have a terribly shameful audacity to be evil. There is a question I ask myself from time to time, and whose answer I do not know with certainty whether we are evil just so we can act tough or if it is something that we do because it is an inborn ability. But this much is certain; we have done things that cannot be justified under the definition of moral beings.

The religious folks with their religious beliefs are right when they say that in every individual resides Satan whispering in the ear, giving ideas, manipulating, and nurturing greed. With committed, working over-hour Satan ideas in collaboration with our geniuses, our malicious actions become inevitable. There are those who do not want to rid themselves of evil, do not seek any reason and compassion for others, and thus are born the lust for war in them, the dominance for mass genocide, and the devastating affliction of killing.

The world, which is the middle of hell and heaven, has become a barbaric slaughterhouse. The act of warfare is as old as time and slowly came into existence with killing. When Cain killed Abel, the wall of Prosperity withholding insane barbarism was breached, the code was cracked, and the game started, or one could say this was the game from the get-go. Was the purpose of our liveliness and peace inclined to war? We killed everything that stood adjacent to our shoulders. The fragility of our ego did not show any clemency to a single living creature that challenged our power. And so began with time the warfare, which grew and grew until it became the intense longing for warriors. The demon was unleashed, war was broken, blood was spilt, humanity was lost, and insanity was discovered.

By no means can we count the wars that have been fought given that all the wars were fought by one being, only that is humans. We have fought for so long for reasons all connected with power. Every being, from the smallest virus to the biggest animal, everything that lives have one thing on its mind, which is survival. Survival has always been our top priority: to live another day, to seek another untold and unknown tomorrow. However, with our need for survival, we deemed it necessary to live another day and to do that, we found it necessary to cut down others. Survival is necessary and everyone right, but by nature, we are terrified to perish and be forgotten like the past. But what is the reason we fight? Is it survival or the masking of our ego? Can we not see another in the same place as us?

The world was divided into races of geographical lineage, and we held our fellow brethren close to us. We have an uncontrollable tendency to protect those we love, specifically those who share a similar heritage and beliefs as us. Back in time, wars were initiated when people from their race were threatened, abused, and killed under the rule of others. Being fair for us is something only a few can achieve, and the reason why it is so hard for us is that there is no bar set for fairness. We cannot be fair; there is always a group that will be offended, so we try to be as moral as possible. Morality gives existence to fairness, so kings and democrats all have an obligation to use their power in morality and harness the fairness people deserve. Fighting to protect and ensure safety, I believe, comes under the definition of moral wars, wars which should be avoided at all costs, but when all doors of reasoning are closed and inhumane trials on humanity are being carried out, then I believe it becomes more of a duty to fight. Fortunately, we live in times where we preach more and more about positivity, from a social media influencer to a politician campaigning for the most powerful position in the world. No matter how fake and false their propaganda for peace is, they have to, for the sake of their position, maintain the positive connotation. In today's world, wars cannot be afforded. With countries having nuclear weapons that are capable of wiping a planet off the face of Earth, it is best to shake hands and reach common ground. Even so, those who still abuse are bought into the limelight through social media.

Since wars were fought to protect, then how come such gruesome mass genocides were carried out? Why do so many innocent lives were lost? How come the moral reason for war turned into a sadistic lust to conquer and expand? Power is a sacred and the most dangerous tool for someone as fragile and volatile as humans. If claimed by those who are blind and unreasonable, then it can only result in bloodshed. No, even something far more sinister than just bloodshed, something that drills the trauma deep in generations. What starts as an honest embark to fairness is soon consumed by the evil desire to conquer what lay bare on others' hands. And soon, with horses saddled, and swords sharpened, the journey begins to expand to the land where the sunsets and everyone who stands in their way is cut down, and the voices of agony and mercy are nullified by the gritty shriek of swords. Ironically the whole idea of expanding through the means of war came into existence from the will to create a safe haven for mankind. The man willed to make a world a spitting image of heaven and exiled mankind from it.

The thought that once came to an 11-year-old boy consumed me in my adventurous days and my dreamy nights. What if we humans had superpowers? Would it be the same fictional scenario? A Superman protecting the world in its entirety? But as I grew, the realization hit like a nightmare that we already were in a world similar to my innocent thought but more tragically realistic. God did not give humans super strength because he knew humans could not survive with an imbalance in force. Look at the world we live in today; we were born with races different from others, and hence we initiated the war of superiority. Heinous and shameful crimes like slavery became common, and the need for supremacy over the other was to maintain egotistical and delusional pride. The man had a fair share of sins he needed to answer, and war was one of them.

Our intellect and free will is a curse that births the idea of sin. Every sin we committed dragged us to the bottomless pit of pride. We are fully aware of sins and the consequences but of all, I believe the real tragedy is the idea of fighting sin with sin. We lie to others before they can lie to us, we talk behind others' backs before they can do it with us, and so we kill others before they can kill us, and all is done so we can survive in this tormented finite space of a time.

Even with the curse of our knowledge, our discoveries, our inventions, and our languages, we still are weak beings who need to hurt others for the validation of their liveliness. I wonder how many people have died in this timeless and shapeless act of war. And for whom have we fought? This barbaric show of power claimed the lives of many innocent people, but even so, war does have its importance. This world that we live in is unjust and unfair, where the powerful take advantage of the weak.

Now to answer the question I put forth earlier, is the man born evil? Or do they believe it to be a necessity in order to survive? I believe a man does have some evil inside of him. A man is born evil, but he is just as evil as he is good. For all that mankind has done throughout history, every inhumane crime we have done has been highlighted gloriously, but every good thing that we have done to make this world a better place, to save this world from disasters, but unfortunately, it did not receive the same reception as evil.

Evil does precede good, which is why we are in this world to show and let every other creation be a witness that even with evil lurking everywhere, we still choose to be kind, show compassion, protect and make this world a better place with every passing moment. There will be evil for as long as we live because it resides within us, but it is we who fight back who refuse unfairness and contain our barbarism. As moral beings, we reflect on our shortcomings and our mistakes and emerge as better beings. That is what being human is like.

Chapter 6: Battles within

A genuine desire to excel oneself and set out on a path that leads to personal development can be found woven intricately throughout the fabric of human existence. This yearning can be a catalyst for personal progress. This never-ending struggle to become better people is profoundly established in the essence of our being. Its origin lies in a natural drive to realise our potential, seek self-improvement, and uncover a sense of fulfilment and meaning in life. In this enthralling investigation, we dig into the intricacies of human nature, illuminating the psychological and philosophical foundations that drive us towards the important goal of pursuing personal development.

Abraham Maslow, the eminent psychologist, unveiled the compelling concept of self-actualization within his iconic hierarchy of needs. As individuals ascend the ladder of human needs, from the primal physiological and safety needs to the loftier realms of love, esteem, and belonging, they are inexorably drawn towards the pinnacle of self-actualization. This pinnacle represents awakening one's latent potential, where personal growth, creativity, and a profound sense of fulfilment converge. Maslow's profound insights illuminate the human drive to continuously strive, reaching beyond our current state and unveiling the extraordinary within.

At the heart of pursuing personal growth lies the mesmerizing allure of intrinsic motivation. Within the depths of our souls, we discover an innate desire to engage in activities purely for the intrinsic satisfaction, pleasure, or personal interest they bring. Liberated from external rewards or recognition, we find joy, paving the path towards personal growth.

This captivating dance of intrinsic motivation fuels our yearning to become the best versions of ourselves, embracing the transformative power of self-directed growth.

The never-ending hunt for meaning and purpose that humanity engages in is inextricably linked to the pursuit of personal development. People proceed on a voyage of self-discovery and development as a result of their in-depth investigations, during which they hone their principles, ideals, and objectives. Pursuing personal improvement turns out to be a tool that helps connect activities with basic beliefs and discover a feeling of purpose that truly resonates within oneself. By working on one's own personal development, one might begin on a significant journey of self-discovery, so giving one's existence meaning and revealing the innermost parts of one's being.

The pattern of one's own personal development unfurls in an infinite variety of ways, each of which reflects the individual's distinct passions and goals. It may involve the development of new abilities, the study of information, the formulation and accomplishment of significant goals, the cultivation of positive relationships, the practise of reflection, the acceptance of personal obstacles, or the courageous pursuit of unique experiences. These expressions of human development are intertwined in a rhythmic symphony, which weaves together the fabric of our ever-evolving personalities.

Pursuing personal growth emerges as an indomitable force within the human spirit, beckoning us towards extraordinary heights of self-discovery and self-improvement. Rooted in our intrinsic nature, it is fuelled by the desire to embrace our potential, discover meaning and purpose, and revel in the inexhaustible depths of personal fulfilment. As we embark upon this transformative journey, cultivating our strengths, expanding our capabilities, and embracing the relentless pursuit of personal growth, we unravel the extraordinary within, illuminating the great fabric of our existence.

Within the intricate tapestry of human existence lies a relentless drive for self-improvement. Since immemorial, the human spirit has relentlessly pursued growth, constantly seeking to surpass its previous limitations. This innate pursuit is imperfect, as humans are bound to make mistakes. Yet, it is through these very mistakes that valuable lessons are extracted, propelling individuals towards an elevated state of being. This insightful discourse delves into the multifaceted reasons behind humanity's unwavering desire for self-improvement. We explore the profound impact of mistakes and the invaluable wisdom they bestow.

The human race, which is distinguished from other animals by consciousness and self-awareness, possesses an innate desire for dominance. Since the beginning of civilization, people have worked hard to improve their levels of education, hone their abilities, and become specialists in a variety of fields. The desire to achieve excellence is profoundly ingrained in the human mind; it compels individuals to push the limits of their capabilities, triumph over challenges, and improve their performance. People are able to pinpoint the areas in which they lack competence, improve their abilities, and move closer to achieving their goals by reflecting on and learning from their past blunders. The constant pursuit of self-improvement that is characteristic of humanity is motivated by a fundamental yearning for happiness and contentment. Every person has their own distinct idea of what makes for a successful and happy life. However, the road to happiness is paved with obstacles and missed opportunities at every turn. Individuals are led in the direction of more fruitful paths through the use of their mistakes, which serve as signposts that illuminate the perils along this difficult trip. One might forge a route towards genuine contentment by engaging in introspection and self-reflection in order to uncover the priceless teachings that lie hidden behind their own erroneous assessments.

An evolutionary urge resides at the centre of human nature and serves as the impetus behind the never-ending quest for self-improvement. Because of the constantly shifting conditions of their environment, human beings have been forced to adapt and develop throughout the course of millennia. This adaptive mechanism is inextricably linked to the bold exploration of one's own capabilities and boundaries. It is important to remember that errors are not failures but rather stepping stones on the path to progress. The collective consciousness is imprinted with the lessons we learn from our mistakes, which shapes subsequent generations.

The human spirit is exemplified by resiliency, endurance, and an unyielding dedication to one's own personal development. Individuals, rather than demoralising them, serve as catalysts for their own personal development when they make mistakes. The essential lessons that may be learned from mistakes are what move people forward and provide them the ability to triumph over challenges with increased resilience and insight. Therefore, the effort to better oneself should be considered an ongoing enterprise. This story, which is always developing, is what makes up the fabric of human existence.

One of the most distinguishing features of humanity is its incessant drive towards self-improvement, which is woven throughout the vast fabric of human history. This amazing drive is propelled by the never-ending search for mastery, enjoyment, and the ability to evolve in response to changing conditions. Individuals discover priceless lessons from their blunders, obtaining insights that not only contribute to their own personal development but also to the collective advancement of society as a whole. We begin a transformative journey towards self-realization and the ongoing improvement of the human spirit when we acknowledge our errors, learn from them, and accept them as a necessary part of our growth.

The complicated web of human life is held together by a profound fact: the force and influence of human connections. This truth is what ties all of us humans together. Our lives are a tapestry that is stitched together with the threads of important relationships ranging from the gentle bonds of friendship to the depths of love and kinship. In this engrossing story, we go out on an adventure to discover the heart of these connections and investigate how they are made, developed, and kept alive. We dive into the complexities of human connections by recounting stories of joy, resiliency, and emotional moments. This is the place where the tapestry of life discovers its greatest meaning.

The enormous maze that life is filled with chance meetings and moments of fortunate timing that work together to bring souls together. These encounters, which may at first appear to be completely coincidental, are actually where the groundwork for human connections is created. The intricate web of fate brings us together with people who make an everlasting impression on our lives, whether it is through the magnetism of kindred spirits, experiences that we have had in common, or shared interests and experiences.

These unplanned meetings go on to form the foundation of meaningful relationships, which in turn mold the course of our lives. Friendship, which may be described as a tapestry woven with laughter, trust, and unwavering support, occupies a unique position in the human experience. True friendships are formed when two people go on experiences together, talk about things that are meaningful to them, and rejoice in one other's successes and failures. Friendship has the power to convert ordinary experiences into extraordinary ones by weaving the paths of two souls together into a tie that cannot be severed. These ties offer solace, support, and a shared journey through the unexpected fabric of life. They might range from childhood buddies to lifelong confidants.

Love, a tapestry imbued with passion, vulnerability, and profound understanding, captures the depths of human connection. From the blossoming of romantic love to the enduring embrace of familial bonds, love weaves its threads through our lives, leaving an indelible impression upon our hearts. Love is an intricate dance of compassion, sacrifice, and unwavering support, nurturing us during times of joy and providing solace in the face of adversity. Through the tapestry of love, we discover the true essence of human connection and its transformative power.

Like any delicate art, meaningful relationships require constant nurturing and care. They are sustained through open communication, mutual respect, and a willingness to invest time and effort. From tender gestures of kindness to acts of forgiveness and understanding, we breathe life into our relationships, fortifying the bonds that weave our lives together. Through the ebb and flow of life's challenges, we learn the art of compromise, empathy, and the beauty of shared growth.

The profound impact of human connections is revealed within the grand tapestry of human existence. From the chance encounters that shape our destiny to the enduring bonds of friendship and love, our lives are enriched by these meaningful relationships. Through tales of laughter, tears, and resilience, we witness the transformative power of human connections, reminding us of our shared humanity and the infinite possibilities. As we nurture and cherish these connections, we perpetuate the beauty of the tapestry, binding our lives together in a timeless embrace.

In the enormous tapestry of human experience, two interconnected realms—personal growth and interpersonal bonds—contribute significantly to the shaping of our lives and the tremendous shifts that they bring about. These realms dive into the core parts of human nature, sparking the never-ending desire for personal development and building relationships that characterise our very existence. Within the pages of this enthralling discourse, we begin on an enthralling trip to uncover the dynamics of personal development and the complexities of human relationships, both of which are sure to excite the soul. We reveal the pathways that lead to self-actualization and meaningful connections by illuminating the essence of our common humanity via the use of moving storytelling and profound insights.

The process of personal development takes the form of an exciting odyssey, inviting us to set out on a life-altering expedition of introspective exploration. It is a never-ending desire that originates from the very centre of our being—a yearning to liberate our full potential, triumph over our constraints, and soar to new heights of personal development. We are able to successfully navigate the maze of our brains by engaging in introspection, self-reflection, and the pursuit of knowledge. This allows us to peel back the layers of our existence and reveal our true selves. This inner journey helps us develop our values, interests, and beliefs, which in turn propels us toward self-actualization and a profound awareness of our place in the world. The capacity to mold our lives and stoke the flames of human connection lies inside the dense web of interpersonal connections, which resembles a delicately woven tapestry. Friendships, love entanglements, familial ties, and the complicated web of societal connections are just a few of the types of relationships that are a part of the kaleidoscope of relationships that characterize our existence.

We discover consolation, support, and camaraderie inside these connections, as well as opportunity for personal development, empathy, and comprehension. To maintain these connections, we need to be vulnerable, listen attentively, and have a compassionate heart. Doing so will enable us to establish unbreakable linkages that are not limited by either time or situation.

We find the profound substance of our common human experience in the depths of our own growth and in the ties we form with others. Our individual and communal potential is unlocked via a commitment to lifelong learning and the cultivation of deep relationships. This fascinating investigation reminds us of the boundless potential we all possess and the immense influence we have on one another's lives. By encouraging one another on our journeys toward self-actualization, we may create a world that is both more prosperous and more closely knit.

The magnificent dance of reciprocal development is revealed as we delve further into the interplay between individual growth and interpersonal ties. Our personal development gets entwined with the betterment of those around us. These life-altering bonds allow us to inspire, challenge, and raise one another up, creating an atmosphere that brings out the best in each of us. These bonds allow us to tap into our full potential as a group and rise to greater heights together.

Chapter 7: Seeking Meaning

In the vast tapestry of human existence, the pursuit of life's purpose has been a perennial quest. Since time immemorial, individuals have sought answers, delving into the realms of religions, spiritual enlightenment, and the inherent will to live. In this book, we embark on a profound journey to understand the significance of these aspects and their distinct roles in shaping the human experience. Through the lens of intellectual exploration, introspection, and scholarly analysis, we unveil the multifaceted nature of our quest for meaning. We lay the groundwork for our exploration by delving into the fundamental question: What is life's purpose? We examine various philosophical and existential perspectives and ponder the significance of purpose in shaping our individual and collective existence. Through a thoughtful analysis of diverse viewpoints, we lay the foundation for our further exploration.

Religion has been a steadfast companion on humanity's journey toward understanding life's purpose. Here, we delve into the religious traditions that have emerged across cultures and civilizations. Drawing upon the wisdom of religious texts, rituals, and teachings, we explore how religions provide frameworks for moral guidance, spiritual growth, and a sense of belonging. We also see the ways in which religion inspires individuals to connect with a higher power, find solace in times of adversity, and discover purpose through devotion and service. Beyond organized religions, the quest for meaning often leads individuals on a personal, introspective path towards spiritual enlightenment.

When, we look in to the ancient and contemporary spiritual practices such as meditation, mindfulness, yoga, and the exploration of consciousness, through these practices, individuals seek to transcend the confines of the material world, connect with their inner selves, and gain insights into the greater mysteries of existence. We know the spiritual enlightenment offers a transformative experience that can unveil one's purpose and foster a deep sense of interconnectedness. Weaving together the insights gained from our exploration of religion, spiritual enlightenment, and the inherent will to live. We understand the distinct purposes served by these aspects in shaping the human experience. Moreover, we live with the potential for synthesis and harmonization, wherein individuals draw inspiration from multiple sources to create a holistic understanding of their purpose. By embracing diverse perspectives and finding common threads, we illuminate the transformative power of an integrated approach to the quest for meaning.

Religions have established themselves as reliable guides within the realm of human spirituality, offering a variety of different ways to traverse the complexities of everyday life. The value of these groups resides in the rich patterns of direction, moral frameworks, and a profound sense of belonging that they provide to people who are looking for a purpose in their lives. The sacred writings, teachings, and venerable leaders of various religions serve as illuminating beacons that shed light upon the ethical landscapes of our existence.

They construct a robust framework that believers adopt in order to chart their route through life's ethical maze through the use of parables, commandments, and ethical principles. Virtues such as compassion, justice, and love find sanctified residence inside these frames, which shapes the moral compass of Christians. Religions offer a haven of clarity in a world that is frequently riddled with moral ambiguity by giving unequivocal advice on how to live a good life. In this way, religions provide a refuge. The human spirit, which is always searching for other people to connect with, finds comfort in the company of others in a community.

People are able to find comfort in one another via the practice of communal rituals and shared belief systems because of the intricate webs of fellowship that are woven by religions. The ability of religious communities to form unbreakable links is the source of their power. Within these communities, believers experience a sense of kinship and purpose that extends beyond their own individual selves.

Believers, when they congregate in holy places and join together in worship and celebration, are able to bask in the warmth of communal connection and find relief from the loneliness that so frequently characterizes our contemporary world. It is within these communities that the seeds of empathy, support, and communal service are planted, and it is here that they grow to full maturity.

There is a sphere of personal development, self-realization, and an unending quest for inner enlightenment that can be found beyond the institutions of organized religions. This ethereal journey encourages the courageous individual to explore inward, where they will discover the limitless depths of their own existence and forge a connection with a reality that goes beyond the everyday.

The journey of self-discovery and development begins for the seeker among the stillness of introspection and reflection on life's meaning and purpose. They excavate the secret recesses of their consciousness by engaging in practices such as meditation, mindfulness, and self-reflection, which results in the discovery of pearls of wisdom and an increased level of self-understanding.

This holy journey enables people to lift the veil of ignorance, which in turn reveals significant insights about their own hopes, concerns, and ambitions. It is a path of self-acceptance, of developing the inner landscape in order to stimulate growth and self-realization, and of fostering the seeds of virtue.

Alongside the investigation of one's own identity, the attainment of spiritual enlightenment throws open the doors to the revelation of a profound connection to something transcendent, something that goes far beyond the confines of one's own unique self. It is an ethereal tapestry that invites the seeker to join with higher awareness, a universal truth that weaves the fabric of creation.

It is beckoning the seeker to combine with this higher consciousness. Individuals can travel the path to connection by overcoming their egos and giving in to the overwhelming majesty of the universe. They get an experience of the oneness that is present across all creation, and as a result, they realize that their own existence is nothing more than a colorful thread in the complex tapestry that is life.

An unquenchable fire, an innate will to live that surges with a vigor that is unrivaled by any other, can be found deep inside the recesses of the human spirit. It is a force that transcends the chains of despair, so transcending the bounds of circumstance and moving us ahead on a constant quest for purpose and fulfillment.

This mysterious essence, which is woven into the very fabric of our existence, arouses an insatiable yearning within each of us to investigate, create, and locate a sense of meaning amidst the enormous tapestry of life. The fundamental drive to live is a formidable ally that stands by our side as we navigate the winding pathways of our earthly journey.

It is a source of relentless motivation that propels us forward and keeps us moving forward. It stokes the embers of curiosity that lie dormant within our souls, compelling us to pursue knowledge, investigate mysteries, and explore new places. Each time we take a step, this power speaks to us in the form of a whisper, reminding us of the limitless potential that lies latent within our being and inviting us to let loose our inner creativity and transform the world around us.

The fundamental drive to life and the yearning for meaning forge an unbreakable relationship deep inside the recesses of our hearts, where they join forces to form an inextricable connection. It compels us to look for a sense of meaning, to try to match our acts with a higher calling that strikes a chord with the very center of our being.

We are motivated by an unquenchable need to contribute, make a difference, and leave an indelible imprint upon the fabric of existence, and as a result, we set out on journeys that might be either heroic or inconspicuous. We discover a sense of fulfillment in our lives when we work towards accomplishing a mission since it is in the accomplishment of a goal that the fire of our innate will to live shines the brightest.

Even if the flame of the intrinsic will to live may flicker in the face of tragedy, it retains an inherent tenacity that defies even the deepest shadows. In times of difficulty, it galvanizes us, filling us with an unflinching desire to conquer challenges and rise above our limitations. It is this spark that kindles hope inside our souls, reminding us that even in the midst of misfortune, life still holds the possibility of transformation, progress, and the realization of our greatest desires.

This hope is what allows us to persevere in the face of adversity. Within the depths of our being is the innate will to live, a steadfast spark that bestows upon us the tenacity to explore, create, and seek out a purpose in life. It is the relentless energy that pulls us ahead, encouraging us to transcend limits, illuminate the world with our own distinctive brilliance, and mold our existence into a masterpiece of tremendous value.

Let us embrace this innate urge to live, stoke its flame, and set out on our path with unyielding resolve, for it contains the core of our human spirit as well as the incredible capacity to influence not only our lives but also the world around us.

Chapter 8: The End of Everything: Death

An average lifespan of a person is around 80 years old, which is roughly 29,000 days. How small is that number considering what an 80-year-old looks like? The wrinkles speak volumes. It looks as if they have been alive for eternity. At least, that's what the frail body says. A person who once was capable of hiking mountains, running marathons, and wrestling giants can now hardly walk. It is truly heartbreaking because those 80 years do not justify that sensation, the pain, and the softness of that physical body.

Our life is nothing short of a miracle, the rarest of the god-composed artistic miracle, which lives and feels transcendental and only lives for less than 100 years. This is something that should necessarily be questioned. It is something that should be presented before the celestial court of God and be questioned with persistence "Why do creatures capable of intellect, capable of making things with the aid of their own mind, live for such a short time?" We can do so much more, make so much more in terms of art, in terms of science, and in terms of creating only if time does not betray us.

For as long as I can remember, I feel like I have lived, seen, and felt enough. Those who live to be old should just be grateful enough to live enough to grow old, considering there are those whose soul is snatched from the body before the body is even wrinkled, before the body draws even the first breath, before the body feels the warmth of a lover, before the body feels the crushing weight of heartbreak.

It is a shame not to fully experience the majestic, divinely gifted human experience after all. But why am I even bothering to ask for a trial when I know well that humans have never been thankful just to be alive? How many times have we on our knees just thanked our maker for creating us? In reality, if anything, we have only cursed our existence.

There are so many who take their own lives, unable to cope with the weight of life. Everyone, including me, at some point, has felt that this existence of ours is not worth enduring and that we have suffered more than eating the sweet fruit of life. Indeed, to live is a gift from God above, a heavenly-composed jurisdiction, but we do not deserve it. However, the same life we cursed through the entire course of our life at the brink of death, we regret it and yearn for more.

That is the centre of our lives, regret. Everyone knows the value of life. We realize how rare this gift is, but we just aren't trained to be grateful, and I believe religion is the only way to do it. Religion makes it a necessity to worship God to be thankful for it.

There is so much to pity for in our existence, and God, too, I believe, pities us. Think about it we are no angels; we have no power to do miracles. We are small creatures who are powerless. Maybe it is for that pity alone that I think God awards us more for the good we do than the evil. Don't we all wonder why are we so hopeless and out of control of our own fate? Shouldn't we have a say in our fate?

Our own beginning, our own end? Was I asked to be born? And will I be asked of death? Will the Angel of Death be so kind as to ask whether I am ready, whether I feel that I have fulfilled my purpose, whether I felt everything there is to feel? It scares me, death. We all fear the inevitable, yet none ever escaped this cruel grasp of the hand that hovers above our heads, the hand that seeks the justification of our sins.

So, what do we make of this powerlessness of our fate? It is not simple. We aren't that innocent, either. We are beings with intellect who know the truth of the world. We are no wanderers of life. As humans, we carry both a job and a moral obligation to lead lives that contribute positively to the world. The circumstances of our birth and the inevitability of our eventual demise are not within our control, and yet we often exhibit a lethargic nature, procrastinating on addressing our challenges and responsibilities until some vague future date.

If we were to possess knowledge of our impending death, we might find ourselves immersed in denial and hostility, or alternatively, we may simply defer the weight of our obligations until our final moments on this Earth. In doing so, we allow the essence of our lives to slip away, leaving behind a hollow existence devoid of significance. The moment of our lives vanishes, and the purpose is betrayed.

Each individual has a defined *time* for themselves. Isn't it worth wondering whether, when we are asked to reflect back on our life, we are taken aback by a small *moment* of our life? This moment does not have a lasting impact on our life, but it is something we think about often in our lives. Perhaps it is the carefree joy of playing baseball with friends, the wind caressing our faces as we pedal our bicycles, or the tender embrace of a first kiss.

Equally, it may be the achingly profound ache of heartbreak, where shattered dreams lay strewn before us. In those shattered fragments, we had envisioned a life intertwined with someone we love, a shared future adorned with a home painted in the hues of love, the echoes of our children's laughter filling the air.

What a poignant lament it is, for we had dreamt of it forever. At age 80, we perceive ourselves to be 16 because that was the *moment* we truly felt alive, and we spent the rest of our lives in that very moment. As time slips by, suddenly, you are on your deathbed, still living off that time when you truly lived. The moment is forever, but how can forever be played in a moment where souls betray the body? In that tiny moment known as *the death*.

From the moment we are born till the day, we will draw our last breath, that small act we play is our whole life. Once the curtain roles and either the clapping or the booing stops, we reflect on whether our performances were good. A stage actor never judges their acting on the claps or the boos. Indeed, they are important and are taken into account, but what really matters is whether the role that was played made any difference. Did they do any justice to the role? If the role was played by anyone else, would it have made any difference?

These are the real questions that consume the actor as he sits in silence, drying their sweat off. Our life which is a play itself, is also the act of convincing ourselves. What starts as a validation-seeking path from others is soon turned into convincing ourselves that our actions, our decisions, our relations, and our emotions are justifiable.

In the end, we began seeking our own validation. Perhaps convincing others is far easier than ourselves, probably because we know more of ourselves than we should know. However, I strongly believe we over-judge ourselves. We make things up about ourselves, things that are not true rumors that destroy us. We do this for our attention. There is a world within us, a universe where every emotion is a planet, and every star is the assumption we make about ourselves.

As the infinite flicker of time passes and as I pay back those precious seconds, minutes, hours, and years that time once lent me, I gradually realize the truth and the fragility of it. The world is composed of individuals who grew up with their own ideals surrounding themselves around the *world* or, more precisely, *their perception* of it. In each one's perception, we have fools, wise, arrogant, smart, beautiful, accomplished, and failures.

We stay in touch with each commonly to take strength from them. For example, we look at unaccomplished and compare them with ourselves whenever we feel down; we compare ourselves with smart people whenever we want to make a decision, thinking, what would they do? We argue with arrogant people whenever we want to feel powerful to bring a change. Indeed, it is a dark side of us, and we do it unconsciously. This is how we live most of our lives in comparison to the people from the world we created and the version we made. But as we get older, we lose the patience and the energy to live in that world anymore.

There comes a certain point in our lives when we tire ourselves, get in touch with reality, and accept it. We reject the world we falsely created. So, in this world, the real one, we seek a change, the truth, and the beauty of it, and once we have it all, we embrace it. Time softens us; it peels off all the layer that stops us from filling the world with color because you realize you don't have time left to argue with fools and arrogant pricks who see the world as a prison of their ideals you let go of them and hope that one day peel their own layers and discover that this life wasn't about proving our worth and enforcing our ideals, but about creating harmony in those we found different to us.

Life was about living with morality, sharing our sorrows, accepting the indifferences, and filling the colorless world with the colors of humanity. At death, we return to the place we came from, so it might be true that as we get closer and closer to our death, we get closer to the real truth.

And as the reaper stands to take away our soul, the whole of life flashes before the eyes, and at that moment, I wonder what goes on in the mind of the soon-to-be-departed, the struggler, the wanderer. Did he enjoy his stay in the Hotel Earth? Will the maker be happy? I keep on wondering, but these wandering are just questions with no answers. And just as it turns out, with time, I do not ponder anymore about death. After all, nothing will stop it. All I can do is find the reality of life and fill it with the colors of my peace.

There is life after death; an audit of our life is only fair. Life after death is the answer to all our suffering, the answer to all the questions we have been asking ourselves. The despair, agony, and turmoil from birth, from battles we fought with ourselves, and battles we fought with others have an end, and it comes after our death. Death is just the last door of questions.

For our light and momentary troubles are achieving for us an eternal glory that far outweighs them all. So we fix our eyes not on what is seen, but on what is unseen, since what is seen is temporary, but what is unseen is eternal.

2 Corinthians 4:17-18

About the Author

Anthony Ravello, hailing from Trinidad and Tobago, has had a life journey of exploring spirituality and growing as a person. He went to Siparia Boys Roman Catholic School, where he learned about Roman Catholicism and developed a strong connection with God. Anthony drifted away from his childhood beliefs in his twenties, but life eventually led him to a new path. Now, he's part of a non-denominational Church that focuses on the teachings of Jesus Christ. They believe that water baptism shows faith in Jesus—a way to express beliefs and obey His example of life, death, and rebirth.

At 67, Anthony's view is inclusive, imagining heaven without divisions between religious groups. He envisions harmony among all souls, whether Catholic, Methodist, or others. Anthony's story reflects growing faith, personal changes, and the power of spirituality on life's journey.

Read more at https://www.anthonyravello.com.